ABI HEADBANGER
A JOURNEY WITH ACQUIRED BRAIN INJURY

STEVEN CLAYSON
WITH
SHARON WELGUS

First published in 2016

Published by Sharon Welgus

Copyright © Steven Clayson and Sharon Welgus

This book is copyright. Apart from any fair dealing for the purpose of private research, criticism or review, as permitted under the Copyright Act, no part may be reproduced by any process without the written permission of the publisher.

ISBN: 978-0-646-93464-8

Cover design: Manfred Quenteschiner
Excerpt from *Geelong Advertiser* used by permission.

Printed by Lulu Online Publishing

ACKNOWLEDGEMENTS

I would like to thank my family and the many friends who have supported me on my journey. I would also like to thank the doctors and health professionals who helped in my recovery. The support of St Laurence services has been on-going and I am very grateful for that. I appreciate the support Anna Loughrey, Sharon Welgus and Manfred Queteschiner have given me to produce this book.

To other sufferers of Acquired Brain Injury, do not let stereotypes hold you back. Get out there and face life!

Steven Clayson

FOREWORD

This book is a gem. Its author Steven Clayson is a gem, a surprisingly uncomplicated man with a particularly complicated introduction into early adulthood. That said - he's also the most gentlemanly trickster I think I've ever known.

Steven and I first met whilst I was employed as a Community Development worker with St Laurence Community Services; a valued colleague, named Michael, introduced him to me. Steven was apparently curious about both my invitation for him to be trained as a 'Living Book' and the idea that he could be loaned out to strangers ('Readers') at a Human Library as part of the 'Blokes Day Out', a community event held in Geelong in 2013.

It came as no surprise to learn that Steven was already in the process of sharing his life story, an endless stream of yarns, with help from his talented and interested neighbor, Sharon Welgus. Privileged to undertake his training, I had full permission to ask Steven about his life, respectfully, just like the readers who would borrow him for 20-minute sessions at the human library event.

In the months leading up to Steven Clayson 'coming off the shelf', Steven shared memorable moments from his life; many enjoyable and others quite terrifying. A central concern for Steven seemed to be that he would not get the chance to be seen for who he really was - highly intelligent and quite hysterically funny. It was through Steven's humour (mostly appropriate) that I unexpectedly learnt how skilful a risk taker he was.

Something else I learnt in conversation with Steven was that just after 'the accident', he feared becoming invisible or worse still that he would be treated like a second-class citizen.

As you read through the yarns that make up this book, *ABI Headbanger,* interwoven with the voice of his friend and creative collaborator Sharon (the narrator), you will experience a mature young man who manages fear differently to most of us. Steven seems to look trouble in the eye; he might laugh for a minute or two (always able to find something funny) and then say to himself, 'I am just going to find my way around this'.

I wonder if Steven knows how many people in his extensive worldly travels have been affected by his disarming honesty and actioned integrity. In these works, you are invited to witness his fight for identity and share his respect for life.

Anna Loughrey
Geelong
April, 2015

INTRODUCTION

My name is Sharon Welgus and I am Steven's neighbor. When I moved to here five years ago, he said hello to me at our adjacent front doors. Very friendly and outgoing, he chatted with me for a few minutes each time we happened to be at our doors. One day, I commented on his Scottish accent and he said he had a motor bike accident a few years ago. His accent had become more pronounced after the accident.

My grandmother was Scottish and I had been to Scotland, so that gave us a starting point. He is a good talker. As I got to know his story over the next couple of months, I was impressed with his courage, resilience and good humour in coping with the legacy of the bike accident. I said one day someone should write his story. He said he didn't know anyone who could do that and I said, 'Well, I think I might be able to do it.'

I had moved to Geelong after retiring from my long career as a secondary teacher. After I retired, I began a course in Professional Writing and Editing at Victoria University. In fact, I was completing the course as I was getting to know Steven. I had also done a lot of History research in the past, including using oral history interviews. I thought I could give it a go.

So, we started. Every week or so, Steven would sit in my lounge room, drink tea (my instant coffee didn't meet his high standards) and eat my biscuits. He talked and I took notes. I typed them and he went through them to make his editing comments. While I've done the writing, these are very much Steven's stories. As far as possible, I've told them in Steven's words, though sometimes I have added my own comments.

The process has been interrupted by some serious health issues on my part, all dealt with now, but Steven has had to learn to be patient. It gave him time to have some more adventures to add to the story.

The better I got to know Steven, the more impressed I am that he has learnt to live independently, travel the world and now looks forward to a happy, settled future. He really is quite a remarkable young man and I hope you enjoy reading his story.

Sharon Welgus
Geelong   2016

1. THE ACCIDENT

Mates
The boys were going to have a few drinks at Steven Kelly's place. Steven Clayson, or Clayson to his mates, lived over the road from his mate, Steven Kelly, and they were going to use the caravan at the back of the Kellys' house. (To help avoid confusion, I will call Steven Clayson 'Steven' and Steven Kelly by his full name.)

It was a Wednesday night in the long January school holidays. Steven had finished Year Ten the year before, which was quite an achievement considering his escapades in and out of school. He had turned sixteen the previous November. Steven Kelly was going to be seventeen in twenty days time. He and Steven were part of a group of friends, the boys, who hung out together in the Corio area.

Of all Steven's friends, Steven Kelly was the most sensible. He was the one Steven felt closest to. Steven Kelly didn't get into trouble at school and was a genuinely nice guy. He loved playing guitar - 'Stairway to Heaven' was a favourite - and the two of them spent a lot of time together. He would go along with what the others wanted to do but he wasn't the one who initiated their plans, generally speaking.

Other friends that came and went that day and night were Marty Rowe, Jason Nicholas and Michael Baulkin. Tim, Steven Kelly's older brother, was also there with his girlfriend, Tanya Mels. The youngest that night was Justin Field, thirteen years old, who was a friend of Tim and Steven Kelly. (1.1)

The boys were regular drinkers in spite of being below the legal age of eighteen years old. It was what they did at the weekends. Somehow someone always found the money for alcohol and the oldest one would buy it at a local bottle shop.

On this particular afternoon, there is general agreement that Steven and Steven Kelly were the steadiest drinkers as they talked and listened to 'Metallica', 'Guns and Roses' and 'Led Zeppelin' in the caravan. In the late afternoon, Jason Nicholas and some of the boys had returned from Corio Village with a slab of Victoria Bitter stubbies, and a bottle each of Jim Beam and Jack Daniels. Steven Kelly had actually been drinking full strength beer throughout the afternoon before he started on the stubbies that evening. Steven was drinking Jim Beam and Coke. Towards midnight, they were both very drunk.

Steven was sober enough, though, to go back to his home briefly. He had a curfew of midnight and his parents were surprised to hear him actually coming in at twelve. In fact, all Steven did was go to his bedroom, put a pillow under the blankets and quietly climb out the bedroom window to go back to the caravan.

Going for a ride
Some of the boys, including Jason Nicholas and Marty Rowe, went home some time after midnight. Then, about 2:00 am, the two Stevens decided that going for a ride on a trail bike would be a good thing to do. Young Justin also wanted to go for a ride with them.

There were three trail bikes kept at the Kelly place. One belonged to Marty Rowe who used to take it over to the paddocks for a ride and he had sometimes let Steven Kelly ride it. Trail bikes are not designed for road use at the best of times, but this bike was unregistered and in poor condition. None of the lights worked, the front tyre was flat and the back brakes didn't work. Steven Kelly still decided to go for a ride on it and Steven decided to go with him. He was the pillion passenger and Steven Kelly was in front wearing the only helmet.

Justin decided to go with them and borrowed Tim's bike, which was registered and in good condition. They headed off on the dark roads, Justin following the two boys.

Steven can't remember exactly where they went. They lived in Corio, a suburb of Geelong. Geelong is built around Corio Bay. In ten minutes driving, though, you can be out in more rural areas. The boys ended up on Anakie Road, heading towards Lovely Banks, which was then an area of small farms and some new housing.

Justin lost sight of them and returned to the caravan. He said it was too dark to see much. Tim thought the boys had probably gone to visit someone. He wasn't too worried.

I don't remember
Steven doesn't remember exactly what happened. These were semi-rural roads, with grass verges, electricity lines and poles but no footpaths. They approached a bend in the road but Steven Kelly didn't see the road turning in the dark. They kept

travelling straight ahead at full speed, ploughing head-first into an electricity pole on the corner.

The impact was so severe that Steven Kelly's helmet split apart and he died instantly from his injuries. Steven was thrown several metres away, landing on his head. He was alive but unconscious.

In the dark, it would be another four hours before anyone would find them. It would be several months before Steven would wake up again.

2. I'M SCOTTISH

'I was a rebel outside of school'
The first thing you notice when talking to Steven is his Scottish accent, though he'll tell you he doesn't have one. He cheers for England when Australia plays cricket against them and follows Andy Murray in tennis tournaments, but he likes to stir the pot, so you never know how serious he is.

Steven James Clayson was born on 21 November 1975 in West Fyfe Hospital, Dunfermline, Scotland. His family lived in Rosyth, a port town on the Firth of Forth, famous for its large dockyard. Although his parents' marriage broke up when he was three years old, and he lost touch with his mother, he had other family members in Rosyth. Eventually his father remarried, and Steven's childhood in Scotland was happy and stable.

He went to Kings Road Primary School, near the Royal Navy Dockyard. Many of his classmates were English, the children of naval staff based in the town. This led to some intense rivalry when Scotland played football against England.

For Steven, football is soccer. His happiest childhood memories are of playing soccer with his mates after school. Primary school in Scotland was also a happy time for him. He even liked his teachers, especially his Grade One teacher, Mrs Stephens. He felt he was achieving well in all his subjects and that he had lots of friends.

'I was a rebel outside of school, though. I was in First Year at Secondary School (Year Seven in Australia) when we were leaving to come to Australia. On my last day, at lunchtime, my friends egged and floured me. I was in such a mess I didn't think I could go into class for the afternoon, so I decided to walk home. That was three miles and walking that far when you are twelve years old is very daunting but it seemed the only thing to do.

'On the way home I walked past a golf course. I noticed there was an old man, asleep on the course near the side of the road. His bicycle was on the ground beside him. So I just took it and rode home. My grandmother lived close to our house and I knew if I rode past her place she would be on the phone to my Dad in no time because she knew I didn't own a bike. So I ditched it near a pub called "The Goth" and walked the rest of the way home.'

In 1988, his family immigrated to Australia. His Uncle Fred had been living in Geelong for some years, working at the Ford factory. Steven's father Ronnie, an electrician, also got a job at Ford with his brother. The family found a house in Corio, a suburb of Geelong and settled down to their new life. That included finding schools for the children – Steven, his step-brother Ronnie and step-sister, Donna.

'Steven won't take a backward step'
Steven's transition to school in Australia could not have been more difficult. It is always hard to settle into school half-way through a school year and even harder settling into a new country. He was small in stature, had a Scottish accent and was passionate about soccer in one of the most passionate Australian Rules Football (AFL) towns in Australia. While there was a local soccer competition, it was not something most Geelong locals took an interest in or were even aware of. He knew nothing about AFL and no-one in his class seemed to know anything about soccer.

He was teased about his accent, teasing that became bullying as far as he was concerned. The bullying happened at lunchtimes and after school, leading to fights at school and elsewhere. He began to get a reputation.

'Steven won't take a backward step,' says Fred, 'and that has always got him into trouble.'

After a few weeks of bullying, Steven decided he needed to deliberately adopt an Australian accent if he was ever going to fit in. Unfortunately, his reputation for fighting had grown and overflowed into the classroom. He would be challenged, he would fight and detentions or suspensions resulted. It was a cycle of behaviour he found hard to stop. His class work was badly disrupted, his relationships with teachers deteriorated and he wasn't getting the results his family knew he was capable of achieving. He felt he was always going to be an outsider.

Soccer seemed to be the only thing he was good at. He joined a local soccer club, and was soon standing out as a top player.

'He could have been anything playing soccer,' Fred says.

Steven also continued to follow his Scottish team, Dundee United, but that wasn't something he could share with friends at school.

A change of school at Year Nine seemed a good idea, but there was little difference in his behaviour at the new school. He never did homework, skipped school and was often defiant towards his teachers. He began to spend time out of school with friends who had access to alcohol. He remembers walking the streets, drinking whisky with them at night. He would even turn up hung over for soccer matches. That didn't impress his coach, but he would still get a game because of his ability.

He was becoming unmanageable. His school didn't know what to do with him and his family was running out of options. He began to take part in illegal activities with some of his mates, petty theft mostly, which led to run-ins with the police and a good behaviour bond in court.

'If it wasn't for the accident, I would have ended up in jail. That's the way my life was going,' Steven says.

Fred agrees that things weren't going well for his nephew.

'It wasn't the friends he was hanging out with. It's just that Steven was Steven.'

He managed to finish Year Ten at school. He was sixteen years old and he didn't really have any plans for the future. He thought he might be an electrician like his Dad and that he would probably end up doing an apprenticeship of some sort. He respected his Dad a great deal.

Meanwhile, it was the summer holidays and having a night drinking with his friends was what he was thinking about.

3. THE AFTERMATH

Finding the boys
Jane Doolan was driving down Anakie Road at 6:15 am on Thursday, 9 January 1992. A horse trainer, she was taking two of her horses in a horse trailer to Geelong Race Course for a gallop. She caught sight of a body and a motor-bike at the side of the road and did a slow U-turn to go back to and check it out. In fact, there were two bodies lying there. A former registered nurse, she could tell that one of the boys was dead and that the other was in a bad way. She flagged down a passing motorist and asked him to call an ambulance, then got some saddle blankets from her car. (3.1)

The motorist pulled into the driveway of William Bond, also a horse trainer and farmer. Bond called an ambulance, hurriedly dressed and grabbed some blankets to take with him.

Steven had been vomiting and was struggling to breathe. Jane Doolan had been unable to turn him on his side but when William Bond arrived, they were able to carefully turn him over and clear Steven's mouth. They put more blankets on him and William Bond kneeled close beside him to use his body warmth to keep Steven warm.

By the time the ambulance arrived, Steven was beginning to have seizures. When the police officers from Corio arrived at 6:35 am, they saw the ambulance officers attending to him, his legs jerking uncontrollably. They called in reinforcements, began taking statements from witnesses and contained the scene. (3.2) Steven was taken to Geelong Hospital.

Inquest
When the inquest was held four months later, the Coroner found that Steven Kelly had died from injuries received when the bike left the road, crossed to the incorrect side and collided with an electricity pole 2.5 metres from the edge of the bitumen. He further found that no person contributed to the cause of death, although excessive alcohol consumption and an unroadworthy bike contributed to the accident. (3.3) Steven had not recovered sufficiently to take part in the inquest.

It was twenty years later that he read the inquest report in preparation for this book. He still has no memory of the accident so reading it helped him to resolve what actually happened that night.

4. HOSPITAL

Head injury
The *Geelong Advertiser* carried the story of the accident on its front page the next morning. 'Dead Boy and Injured Mate Lie by the Road for Four Hours' was the headline.

'A teenage trail bike rider died and his 16 year old pillion passenger lay critically injured on the roadside for more than four hours at Lovely Banks early yesterday... The critically injured youth suffered head injuries. He was rushed by ambulance to Geelong Hospital....Police bids to identify the youths were hampered yesterday because there was no identification at the scene.' (4.1)

All Steven had on him was a wallet with no identifying documents; there was just a photo of his ex-girlfriend, Chelsea, in it. One of the police officers thought he recognised her but it was late afternoon before they tracked down her address and went to her home to see if she knew who would have her photo in their wallet. They then notified the families.

Fred's wife called him at work where he was doing overtime. He left straight away and he and his wife rushed to the intensive care unit at Geelong Hospital to join Steven's parents, Ronnie and Frances.

The doctors at Geelong Hospital had placed Steven in an induced coma. He was connected to tubes and equipment via a tracheotomy to help him breathe.

He had critical brain injuries and was continuing to have seizures. He had also broken his left collarbone and some bones in his hand. The doctors said they would have to let his injuries stabilise before they could see the extent of the damage done. It was obviously very serious.

His family was devastated. They began a daily vigil at the hospital, waiting for him to come out of the coma so the doctors could tell them the extent of the damage.

Steven Kelly
At the same time, they knew Steven Kelly and his family, so they were grieving for their loss as well. From the Friday after the accident, moving tributes appeared each day in the *Geelong*

Advertiser from Steven Kelly's family and friends. The Clayson family's tribute read:

'KELLY, Steven – Will always be remembered in our eyes. Still asleep in hospital, we know Clayson is thinking of you. Sadly missed – Clayson family. Ronnie, Frances, Steven, wee Ronnie and Donna.' (4.2)

Steven Kelly's memorial plaque at Geelong Eastern Cemetery.

Twenty years later, I gave Steven some photocopies of the tributes. The tears began to flow as he read them, even though he had assured me that reading the tributes after all this time wouldn't upset him. It was filling in the emotional gaps for him, catching up on what he wasn't able to experience at the time.

Awake but not really
Once Steven came out of the induced coma, he was moved out of intensive care to a room in a ward. He was still unconscious, his eyes closed. Doctors encouraged the family to do all they could to stimulate his mind, so they brought in a cassette player and played his favourite music, talked to him and read to him. Fred read the soccer results to him from the local paper.

He opened his eyes two weeks after the accident but he was far from 'awake'. Only part of his brain was responding.

Steven was given a video of collated film clips made by friends and family members from this time so that he would have a record of a period of his life that he would not remember. In the earliest clip, he is curled up in a foetal position in a chair, his eyes closed. In the next one, he is lying on his bed, propped up on pillows, still with a tracheotomy inserted in his neck and a nasogastric tube connected. His friend Jason is filming; he asks Steven to smile but he makes no response. Steven is looking but not seeing. Finally, he moves his leg when Jason asks him to, but still shows no sign of recognising any of the family and friends in the room.

Ronnie wipes his son's face, cleaning gently around his mouth and nose and wiping his hands. Steven just stares straight ahead. There is a white board on the wall beside the bed covered in messages from his friends and family. Also on the wall are Metallica and Dundee United posters beside his Dundee United jumper and tee-shirt. At the bottom of the white board, '22 days' is written in large letters.

The camera moves to two girls sitting by the bed. They are Steven's friends, talking quietly to each other, occasionally speaking directly to him, but he just looks blankly at them. He occasionally moves his legs or looks around the room, but that is the only movement he makes. Today, he has no memory of any of this.

After three weeks at Geelong Hospital, Steven was moved to the Rehabilitation Centre at Bethesda Hospital in Richmond, an inner-city suburb of Melbourne. This well-regarded centre specialised in the type of long-term rehabilitation Steven was going to need but its location was an extra burden for his family.

Whether you drive from Geelong by car and then through the busy city centre of Melbourne to Richmond, or whether you take public transport, it is a three hour return trip. Yet Steven's family continued to visit him every day. Fred remembers offering to go alternate days during the week so Ronnie and Frances could have a break.

'I thought I'd been kidnapped'
Steven was in a special bed with deep padded sides because of his epileptic seizures, called a Cray bed at the hospital, as he recalls. One day, after about three months at Bethesda, his family got a telephone call to say that he had "woken up". Steven tells the story.

'When I first woke up, I stood up in the bed with high sides so I could look out but I fell over. I tried to vocalise what I was thinking but I couldn't talk. My brain didn't remember how to push air out when I wanted to speak. I was just moving my lips. I remember putting my finger against my temple and thinking, "I'm spastic!" That's not a term I would use now, but I was only sixteen and didn't know any better. I thought I'd been kidnapped and when the doctors came, and asked me questions like "What's your name?" I froze and couldn't answer, even though they gave me a spelling board to spell out my answer.

'They called my family to say I was awake and I was very happy to see some familiar faces at last.

'It took six months of intensive rehabilitation for me to learn to eat, talk and walk again. I spent six to eight weeks in a wheelchair. In my mind, a wheelchair equalled disability and restricted my plans to succeed in life. I used to hoist myself up on the edges of the Cray bed and walk around the bed, exercising my muscles. I even pulled out my naso-gastric tube so I could move about more. I was determined to walk again. I was not going to be confined to a wheelchair.'

His days were filled with physiotherapy, occupational therapy and speech therapy sessions. In the afternoons, he had to sleep for a while before getting ready for family visits. His epilepsy was under better control and his memory was improving all the time, though he would occasionally have bouts of post-traumatic amnesia.

He was impatient to eat again:

'I just wanted the sensation of eating. It's strange to think of that now.'

It really hurt when they reinserted his naso-gastric tube, but he had to use it. It took long sessions with a speech therapist before he could eat by himself again. On one occasion, Steven had a visitor while a fellow patient was away having therapy. He saw the morning tea left on the patient's side table waiting for his return, a lamington on a plate. Steven pushed his visitor out of the way to get the lamington.

'I choked a bit on the coconut but I enjoyed the sensation of moving my jaws to eat again. It felt great.'

Frustration
Teenagers aren't known for their patience. Steven was a feisty sixteen-year-old before the accident and now he was a feisty sixteen-year-old with a brain injury. As a result of that injury, he was compulsive in his behaviour, very emotional, a little paranoid and he had a short attention span. He was also frustrated at the slowness of his recovery.

On his DVD, there are clips of his therapy sessions at Bethesda. On a clip dated 4 June 1992, he is kicking a soccer ball in the passage of Bethesda. He looks very young and baby-faced, even for a sixteen-year-old, with blonde streaks in his hair. He keeps dribbling the ball like a naughty boy even though a voice is asking him to stop so they can film him walking. When he speaks, you can recognise the voice as his but it is hard to understand him. What he says clearly is that rehab is boring.

'What I was really trying to say is that I was frustrated I'd been put in a position where rehab was necessary.'

He loses focus quickly and wanders off but comes back and walks when they ask him to.

Another clip shows Steven with a female speech therapist and in this clip he is much more cooperative. During the interview, Steven says that he thinks he is going home in a couple of weeks. He keeps yawning when the therapist speaks to him. She asks him how long he has been at Bethesda and he says, 'Too long!' Then she asks him what he remembers about the accident. 'I was drunk', he replies. He says he doesn't really remember the accident.

He recites the speech therapy activities he needs to practice and talks about the soccer book he is reading. His words come slowly, one at a time. She talks about how difficult he found it to talk when they went for a walk outside a few days ago, one word per breath, and that he had trouble raising his voice above the traffic. Steven says he is still having trouble pronouncing 'b', 'p' and 'd'.

His Scottish accent is strong. He tells her about his local soccer club that is having a fundraiser to help him get an exercise bike and clothes that he needs. You have to concentrate to follow him but at least he is talking: when he laughs, it is just like he laughs now, and he laughs a lot.

Unless you have been through it yourself or with a family member, it is hard to imagine how much work is needed to retrain an injured brain so that the person can walk and talk again. Therapists and patients need to be patient and persistent. The on-going support of families is essential. For Steven, the incentive was to get back to who he was before and to go home. He wanted to be normal again, to fit in with his friends and not be someone with a disability. It took time, a long time for a teenager.

Family
His family continued to visit regularly but it was hard for his friends to get there. Apart from the travelling time, their lives had moved on. Steven didn't encourage them because he didn't want them to see him struggling to do things or treat him as someone who was disabled.

He had wondered why his mate Steven Kelly hadn't been to see him. His family thought it best not to tell him about his death at first and waited until six months after he "woke up". He was very emotional when he heard the news and grieved for some time.

In September, 1992, nine months after his accident, Bethesda thought he was ready for his first home visit. To begin with it was just day visits and then he began to stay over for weekends. For Steven, nothing about his home seemed to have changed, but his family had got used to not living with him in the house. It was challenging for all of them when he went home permanently in October: everyone had to make adjustments. He was still very impulsive, emotional and paranoid. He was also still a rebellious sixteen-year-old.

Dealing with his epilepsy was a learning curve for his parents. He could have a seizure at any time and that was stressful for them. They were very protective of him but Steven resisted this. For example, he still needed to use a wheelchair for trips outside the house but there was no way he wanted to be seen by his friends in a wheelchair. There were many arguments.

By Christmas time, his family had decided that the best thing for everybody would be for Steven to complete his rehabilitation somewhere else. They decided on Ivanhoe Manor, a long-term rehabilitation facility in the north-eastern suburbs of Melbourne.

5. IVANHOE MANOR

I was a very angry person for a while
Steven tells the story.
'I moved into Ivanhoe Manor Private Rehabilitation Hospital in Ivanhoe, a north-eastern suburb of Melbourne, at the end of 1992. Most of the people there were in their thirties, so I was one of the youngest. I progressed to a semi-independent unit sharing with one other man. We shared a kitchen but we each had our own bedroom with an ensuite bathroom. We were supposed to do our own cooking but I was too impatient to cook. Mostly I bought takeaway, but sometimes I would try and con a meal from the hospital kitchen. We also did various workshops, went on organised outings and continued having physiotherapy and occupational therapy.

'I used to go to speech therapy sessions at Latrobe University and I was infatuated with the student worker who took my sessions. (I have met her since that time and we had a laugh about it over a beer.)

'I was able to play some soccer with a local team, the Kew Deaf Soccer Club, and on the weekends I went home for visits. For exercise, I also used to walk from Ivanhoe Manor to Northland, which is a fair distance.

'I was a very angry person for a while. I don't remember being angry about what had happened to me. That was just how things worked out as a consequence of my rebellious behaviour. It was more that I lost my temper very easily. I beat up my housemate in the unit. Ivanhoe arranged some anger management sessions and that helped a lot.'

Eighteen and it's New Year's Eve
'I turned eighteen in November, 1993. When I was home at Christmas time, my father introduced me to some of the hotels in Geelong but I decided to go back to Ivanhoe for New Year's Eve. I said to myself, here I am, eighteen on New Year's Eve, and stuck in a hospital. I waved to the nurses and said I was going out to the pub.

"'Which one?" they asked.

"'The Old England in Heidelberg,"' I said. They knew I was headstrong and confident so they didn't try to stop me.

"'Come straight back when you're finished,"' they said.

'"Yeah, okay," I said. So I caught a taxi to the hotel. I had a good time for a while. Then I walked out the back of the hotel and jumped in a taxi that was just sitting there.

'"Take me to a nightclub!" I said, so he took me to into the city to the Warehouse nightclub in South Yarra, just off Toorak Road.

'It was a bit of a "druggie" nightclub at the time but I didn't know that. I'd never been to one before. After walking around, trying to find a group I could fit in with, and buying a couple of drinks, I left.'

Getting bashed
'Two people followed me from the nightclub, a girl I had been talking to at one of the bars and her boyfriend. They followed me down Toorak Road, offering me a lift home and sticking around. They weren't scaring me, I wasn't frightened but I knew something was wrong. I began to think they were up to something.

'I was begging people who walked past, "Please help me! Please help me! They're weird!" But it was New Year's Eve, people were doing their own thing and they didn't want to know. Who knows what they thought of me?

'I came to a telephone box on Toorak Road and rang Ivanhoe Manor, told them where I was and they said, "Don't move! We'll send a taxi!" Then the couple came along and convinced me I would never get a taxi there. I kept walking, then, to get away from them as much as I could.

'Anyway, they finally got me in a parking lot down the road. They got me down on the ground and were kicking into me, with full blows to the head. I curled up in a ball to protect myself and managed to keep my awareness. They took my shirt, my tee-shirt, my wallet, my asthma spray and all my change-even my belt. People didn't have mobile phones then.

'Because I'd kept my awareness I was able to follow them when they finally walked away, but in the dark I lost them. I was saying to myself, "Shit! Shit! Where did they go?", when someone grabbed me from behind and got me in a headlock.

'"Where do you think you're going?" they said, but I threw them off.

'"I'm going home, leave me alone! I'm going home!" I said over and over but they walked me down to a bridge over the Yarra River. They kept asking me for my PIN number but I was too distressed and had lost the power of speech. Finally, when I could speak again, I gave them a false one. They told me to take my trousers and everything off and they were going to push me over the edge.

'I was thinking, "Shit, this is scary. I'm in trouble here." I grabbed onto the steel railing, pushed myself back up, spun around and said, "Right! That's it! I'm finished with this! Me-you-now! One-on-one! Forget her!" I punched him on the chin and he stepped back to think about the situation. I don't think he could believe I wanted to fight. I didn't want to fight him - I was just buying time after the kicking I'd taken. I had no money left but at least I had my wits. I just wanted a chance to run.

'So, while he was thinking about it, I ran, but he caught up with me and dragged me to the other side of the river. They were kicking into me again. A guy walked past and I yelled out, "Help me! Help me!" He turned around to look, paused, but then he just kept walking. When he turned around, they watched him and I had another chance to run. I managed to get away and hide in some bushes. In the darkness, they couldn't find me. I stayed hidden for maybe half an hour or more.'

You're an idiot!
'When I came out from the bushes, I found two people, a couple, who I thought might help me. They were walking home and offered to take me to their place. When I noticed the man was wearing the same boots as the guy who attacked me, I panicked. They say that after a traumatic incident, the next people you see look like the perpetrators. But then I calmed down and realised they were different. The lady especially was very kind. The man asked me, "Do you want me to ring your mum and dad?"

'I said, "No, could you ring the hospital I'm in?" He was shocked, asking me what I was doing out. "I'm eighteen and I'm not spending New Year in hospital," I told him. Looking back now, I think that's really funny. I have no idea what they were thinking they'd come across.

'When I eventually got back to Ivanhoe, the male nurse on duty kept saying, "You're an idiot! You're an idiot!"

'"Leave off!' I said. "You don't even know what happened. I know what happened."'

"You're a smart-arse!" he replied.

'There didn't seem to be any permanent damage from the kicks to my head. I had scratches and bruises all over me, but I've taken a few beatings in my life and I've had worse. Because I had been rebellious, I had been in a few fights and I actually don't mind a good hit-out.'

Compensation
'My father came the next day and took a photo of all my bruises. Automatically, I smiled. "Don't smile, you idiot!" he said.

'In the weeks after, one of the nurses at the hospital who had had a bit to do with crime compensation in the past said to me, "Why don't you go to the police?" I called them and they sent around a detective to see me. He had a book of photos and asked me to see if I could identify which one it was. When I saw the man's photo, I knew without a doubt. The detective wanted me check the rest of the photos to be sure, but I was positive that he was the one.

'It went to court and he and the girl each got 36 hours of community work.

'A legal representative went with me to the Crimes Compensation Court. I had a bit of a dispute with the judge. He said, "Who do you think you are, going out by yourself on New Year's Eve, such a dangerous night to be out, when you are meant to be safely in a hospital?"

'I said, "Excuse me, but I believe that anyone has the right to go out at any time and feel safe and not be set upon by people like that."

'My legal representative whispered, "Shut up! You're winning!" I said I knew what I was doing and in the end I was awarded a lot more than I lost.'

Steven continued at Ivanhoe Manor, becoming more confident and independent with each month he spent there. He was able to travel home by train for occasional visits and could manage his money without any problems. It was time to take more responsibility for his life.

6. INDEPENDENCE

I made the decision myself
Steven continued to improve and enrolled in a work training program designed to prepare young people from various backgrounds for employment. Increasingly, Steven was feeling restricted at Ivanhoe Manor. Mixing with other young people on the course increased his desire to take responsibility for himself and live a normal life.

Steven explains:
'I was taking part in a Landcare Environment Action Program (LEAP), a work training program, travelling by train from Ivanhoe Manor to where the course was held at Epping College of Technical and Further Education (TAFE).

'One day, I decided that no-one at the hospital was going to tell me when it was time to go out alone, so I made the decision myself. When I got off the train each day, I walked past a real estate agent's office. One weekend, I returned and asked about renting a unit. I looked at several flats over the next few weeks but none of them appealed to me. Finally, the agent got fed up with me and he said the next one he showed me, I had to take or else go to another agent. It turned out to be okay, in a good location near the train station, and I said I'd take it.

'I had to do a lot of persuading. I had trouble providing identification documents because I'd been an inpatient since just after I was sixteen. The real estate agent had checked with my Occupational Therapist at Ivanhoe Manor that I was who I said I was. The people at Ivanhoe Manor, the Transport Accident Commission (TAC) who provided some of my support and my parents all advised me not to do it but I knew I had to.

'I knew if I stayed at Ivanhoe I would just stagnate. I was eighteen and wanted to be as fully independent as I could be. Financially, I had received a settlement from the Transport and Accident Commission after the accident. My father and my Uncle Fred were my trustees. I always got money from them when I asked because they knew I was responsible with money. I had made the decision and it was what I was going to do.

'I moved into the unit in Rosanna and started looking after myself on 18 September, 1994. I bought everything I needed for the unit and arranged for it to be delivered the day I moved in. Absolutely everything was new.

'There were no support services that I recall, such as home help, for six to eight months. I no longer had any involvement with Ivanhoe Manor and managed my life by myself. I cooked my own simple meals or bought takeaway – I think I ate a lot of pizzas and baked beans. I did what I had to do.

'It was lonely at times but I knew I could persevere. There was always something ahead. Maybe not all eighteen-year olds could do what I did, but I really enjoyed being able to do it and stepping out of the "disability" stereotype. I wanted to keep moving forward.

'During weekdays, I continued to attend a Work Training Project at Epping TAFE and that lasted for six months. The friends I had were people I met on the course. I didn't really have any friends in the local area where I lived.'

Living independently and attending a course were huge steps in Steven's recovery. Managing the symptoms of his brain injury took a lot of courage and this would be a good place to look at those symptoms in more detail.

Brain Injury
This is the definition of a brain jury by the Brain Injury Association of Australia:

'Acquired brain injury - or "ABI" - refers to any damage to the brain that occurs after birth, with the exception of Foetal Alcohol Spectrum Disorder (FASD). That damage can be caused by an accident or trauma, by a stroke, a brain infection, by alcohol or other drugs or by diseases of the brain like Parkinson's disease. Brain Injury is common. Over 600,000 Australians have an acquired brain injury. Three out every four of them are aged under 65. As many as two out of every three of these people acquired their brain injury before they turned 25. Three out of every four people with acquired brain injury are men.' (6.1)

I recommend the Brain Injury Association website for its clear explanations and useful fact sheets. There are many other organisations that seek to help people with brain injuries and several are listed in 'Useful Links' at the end of this book.

An important thing to understand is that brain injury differs from intellectual disability:

'Acquired brain injury is a complex and individual condition...(It) is distinct from intellectual disability. People with a brain injury may have difficulty controlling, coordinating and communicating their thoughts and actions but generally retain their intellectual abilities.' (6.2)

Getting other people to understand this difference is very challenging for people with an ABI, especially since the individual symptoms will differ from one person to another.

Managing the symptoms
There were a range of symptoms Steven needed to manage. For example, at times he could be immature and impulsive in his decision making. That isn't necessarily unusual for young adult men but some aspects of his emotional development had been delayed by his accident. He believes his capacity to remember things was excellent but that at times he had a shortened attention span. The anger management strategies he had learnt at Ivanhoe were effective and he had learnt to recognise paranoia in his thinking and deal with it.

Steven had learnt to manage his epilepsy. He knew the symptoms of an approaching seizure and could put himself in a safe place, calling an ambulance if necessary. Physically, he didn't have full use of his left arm and some small motor movements were difficult. His gait and his sense of balance were affected, but he was a strong, fast walker who could walk several kilometres a day.

He had a speech impediment because of damage to his neck and face muscles so his speech could be a little slurred at times. As well, the Scottish accent of his childhood had become more pronounced. This sometimes made it hard for people to understand him until they realized it was a Scottish accent they were listening to. He had a very weak sense of smell which could be an issue with cooking, but he says that since he had no motivation to cook, that wasn't a problem.

What Steven had retained was all his intellectual capacities, which having an ABI doesn't affect. He was quick-witted, funny, articulate and well-informed, able to hold his own in any conversation. He was a good manager of his own money, and his father and uncle who acted as his trustees never had concerns in that area. He was fiercely independent, determined and defiant towards the limitations he lived with or which people assumed of him.

One area where he was not so responsible was in drinking too much alcohol, which he freely admits now. Again, like many young adult men, his points of social contact were hotels and clubs. It was where he could meet up with other people his age.

In these social situations, there was always the challenge of pressing on past initial impressions of what his disabilities might be. He made some good friends but also had to learn to handle negative reactions.

He also felt a strong responsibility towards others who had an illness or disability. Steven's story about his friend Paul gives an insight into how Steven was at this stage in his life.

Paul
Steven met Paul through friends he made while doing his second LEAP course.

'Paul had epilepsy and used to smoke marijuana. One night, we were at a mutual friend's place. Paul sculled a whole bottle of Galliano, a liqueur, drinking in shots over an hour. Then we all decided to catch a train and head for the Baghdad Hotel in Collingwood, now called the Peel Hotel.

'Paul passed out on the train. There were cops on the train and they wanted to take him into custody but I argued with them, saying I'd take responsibility for him. They agreed to this so we got him out at Victoria Park, the next station. We called a cab but the driver refused to take him alone because of the state Paul was in. Someone had to go with him so we went around my mates and we all said no, we wouldn't, the first time around.

I had only just met Paul and didn't know much about him. What I did know was that he had epilepsy so I knew I had to look after him. The second time around, I said I would go with him. So, Paul and I headed for St Vincent's Hospital in the city and I arranged to catch up with my friends at the Cadillac Bar in Swanston Street.

'The driver helped me carry him into emergency and I gave what little information I knew about him to reception. Then four or five staff rushed him off. The staff in the emergency room wouldn't let me in to see him so I punched a concrete pillar. I'd been drinking too and I was a bit confrontational. Very confrontational! I told him they could tell his family I left him outside on the road if they wanted as I didn't want to spend the whole night at the hospital.

Steven and Paul

'So I left and went to the Cadillac Bar. I had to argue my way in, explaining to them that I had a brain injury. Then I walked around in circles, drinking heavily and looking for my friends. Finally I saw them at the bottom of the steps outside and I ran down and put my arms around Dave whom I'd met on the Greensborough course, saying, "I love you!" They were embarrassed and told me to cut it out.

"Thank-you for sticking by me," I said, "for turning up and being loyal." I value loyal friends.

'I met up with Paul years later in Brisbane and we are still good mates. The hospital actually did tell his family I left him outside and he still thought that's what I did. I told him I was disappointed he would think that. If the cops on the train had locked him up for the night, he would have died in his cell, according to the medical staff in the hospital, because of his blood alcohol level.'

Confrontational
As in this story, Steven admits he was often very confrontational with authority figures when he had been drinking, sometimes using his brain injury as a justification for his behaviour. This was better than being labeled as just drunk in terms of the consequences he might face. It is very difficult for police and protective services officers to tell the difference between those who have a brain injury

and those who are inebriated or on drugs. Of course, people may be both.

Things didn't always go well with him in his contacts with the police. One example of this occurred when Steven was out with a friend in Melbourne. Steven and his friend were trying to enter a venue but the bouncer barred them. They argued with him and the bouncer ended up kicking Steven in the stomach. The police arrived. When one policeman pushed Steven's friend, Steven saw red and pushed back at the policeman. Another policeman dragged Steven along the ground and slammed him into the back of a divisional van. He had some epilepsy tablets but they were taken off him when he was put in the lock-up. He was kept there for four hours and then released.

Several months later, a letter arrived in regard to a missed court appearance. Steven contacted a disability discrimination centre and spoke to a lawyer, saying his medication had been taken from him. His lawyer contacted the police and the case was dropped.

There is no doubt that Steven would have presented as inebriated and confrontational to the police. On the other hand, it is not helpful for police treatment to include further damage to the head or for medication to be withheld. These are challenging situations for police to deal with. The tendency to be more emotional and impulsive that can come with an ABI is made worse by alcohol. Not surprisingly, people with brain injuries are over-represented in homeless groups, in those involved with the criminal justice system and those with serious alcohol or drug dependent problems (6.3).

Loneliness is the price you pay
These are the issues Steven was dealing with as he lived in his unit in Rosanna for the next two years. Some of the first friends he met were on the LEAP course he completed at Epping TAFE, a program for people who were on the long-term unemployment list. They were social friends he would sometimes meet up with, usually to go to the movies or to a rave dance party. The course didn't lead to a job for Steven. Most of the time, he spent his evenings alone in his unit in Rosanna, watching television. He thinks he was very reclusive for the next two years, believing that loneliness was the price he needed to pay for independence.

He visited his family in Geelong at weekends, travelling by train. He sometimes met up with former friends but they had moved on with their lives. He went to local soccer games and he would occasionally go out for a drink with friends at his favourite pubs.

He maintained a link with Ivanhoe Manor, calling in to visit the people he knew there. However, he was no longer a patient so he didn't receive any medical support from them. He had a local doctor he saw to manage his epilepsy but otherwise was coping with life by himself without the support of any other agencies.

In 1997, two years after his first LEAP course, he received an invitation from Epping TAFE to do a second LEAP course. He met a mate on the course who needed somewhere to stay, so he moved in with Steven for a few months. This friend had some issues that made him hard to live with and in the end Steven had to ask him to move out.

It was time for a change
With no jobs resulting from the course, Steven felt he needed a change of situation. He wanted to travel, to revisit his childhood in Scotland and catch up with friends and family. He wanted to try out back-packing and was confident he could

manage it. He packed up his belongings, put them into his Dad's garage and went to Scotland for a year.

For the next few years, Steven alternated between travelling and working. It seemed simpler to collect the travelling stories in one chapter and the work stories in another. The next chapter, Chapter Seven, tells the story of Steven's working life. His travelling stories are collected together in the following chapter, Chapter Eight.

7. GETTING A JOB

Making a contribution
Travelling was very empowering for Steven. He returned in 1999 determined to make life work for him. He rented a unit in Corio, not far from his family, and began looking for a job.

He had enough money to live on so income wasn't his motivation for working. He wanted a sense of purpose and to be able to make a contribution to life. Travelling had increased his confidence and willingness to try new experiences. Centrelink (run by the Department of Human Services) referred him to a disability job employment agency called 'Tap into Employment' (TAP), operated by St Laurence Community Services.

St Laurence Community Services are a not-for-profit charity group formed in 1996 to take over the community services previously provided by the Brotherhood of St Laurence in the Geelong region.(7.1) The Federal Government had recently created Job Networks to outsource employment services from Centrelink, and St Laurence Services had moved into this role in the area of disability employment services.

Steven wasn't exactly 'work ready'. He was now 24 years old and had never really worked before. His years at secondary school had been patchy in terms of his education because of absences and behaviour problems. The accident happened at the end of Year Ten and Steven concedes he had barely passed that year. Apart from the two LEAP courses, he had been in rehabilitation, travelling or doing his own thing in his own time for the last eight years.

Steven tried a few jobs suggested by TAP but they didn't work out, so he left them. The people at TAP were getting frustrated with Steven because nothing ever suited him. Finally, a job was advertised at 'Happy Hens', a poultry farm at Meredith. Steven decided this was a job he would like. He telephoned the TAP number every half hour until they finally agreed to give him a referral to the job.

He got the job and stayed for two and a half years until the farm had a quarantine situation related to the chickens and had to close down for several months. Steven's life was very stable while he worked there. His disabilities didn't affect him at all in doing the job, there was a good working environment and he was only drinking at weekends for most of his time there.

However, towards the end his drinking increased. 'It was a way of making social contacts,' he says. 'It wasn't so much the need to drink alcohol.' One consequence of too much drinking for him was weight gain, which was not good for his health.

While 'Happy Hens' was out of action he decided to try another job at 'Shellac Attack', a spray painting firm in Newcomb, Geelong. Steven admits he wasn't very good at it and he got sacked after a few weeks.

TAP then sent him to a job on a tomato farm just out of Geelong but Steven found the attitude of the woman in charge very offensive in relation to his disabilities. He walked out after one week.

A mate he knew from the LEAP course was having some serious issues and came to live with Steven for a short time. He spent time trying to help his mate and stopped looking for jobs altogether. As his mate improved, he started to think about travelling again.

'If someone came and offered me a job now that I thought I could do, then I would take it. It's an uphill battle to get employers to see someone for what they can offer, not for what they can't offer. The knock-backs hurt too much. I just want to be treated with respect. I wouldn't waste someone's time if I thought I wasn't up to the job.'

Apart from a three week job several years later, at a time when Steven was in a bad place, he has not worked since this period of his life.

For a time, travelling overseas gave him a focus in life. It extended his friendships and developed his confidence, but he always had to come home again.

The next chapter, Chapter Eight, tells the story of his travelling experiences.

8. TRAVELLING

Going back to that childhood time
Steven's first trip overseas was to Scotland in 1997.

'Going to Scotland changed everything for me. My family and friends didn't think I could do it, but I organized everything myself – tickets, passport, money, accommodation. I wanted to prove I could do it. It was very empowering.'

He didn't really remember the relatives he had there. It was more about catching up with his school friends. He had stayed in touch with them since leaving for Australia. His family in Geelong was concerned about how he would cope, but at least he would be in a place they knew and where they could ask relatives to keep an eye on him.

Steven flew via Osaka, Japan, to London, then on to Edinburgh where his friends met him. He stayed in his home town of Rosyth, which is not far from Edinburgh.

'Rosyth had hardly changed at all and I remembered where everything was.' The disappointment for him was in realising that things had moved on as far as his friends were concerned. He wasn't revisiting his childhood as he had hoped. He did enjoy catching up with his friends, though, and managed to visit some family members in Glasgow and Dundee.

Cousins Lesley and Shaun

'It's a different lifestyle over there. People go to the pub seven days a week.' He was drinking, watching soccer and catching up with the lifestyle of his friends. In hindsight, he thinks he wasted a lot of time going to soccer matches. It was all about trying to relive childhood memories of going to the soccer with his family and mates.

Football matches were on at weekends, so he did some sight-seeing around Scotland and England during the week. He also took a trip to Ibeza, an island off the coast of Spain.

Every day, he telephoned home to check that everything was okay. Part of the paranoia that came with his ABI was that things might change at home while he was absent.

Although he was drinking a lot, he wasn't so comfortable with other activities some of his friends were into.

'While I was staying in Rosyth, my mates wanted to take me to a strip show club. I said okay as long as you don't try and embarrass me. When the girl started dancing, my mates must have been pointing me out because she came over to me and tried to get me up to dance with her. I actually feel quite shy in those sorts of situations and when she saw on my face that I was uncomfortable about it she went on to choose someone else.'

Another time, Steven saw a 'wee' boy in the street kicking a football.

'I got the ball off him, dribbled it around him a few times then gave it back. I wanted to play with him, be a child kicking a football in the street again, but he was scared of me and ran off. I just couldn't go back to that childhood time.'

After several months in Scotland, Steven went back to Australia.

'I realized I would always be Scottish, but Australia was my home now.'

He returned more confident in his own abilities and set up a unit in Corio, near his family, and worked in paid employment off and on for the next few years. In 2003, when he was 27 years old, he was ready to travel again but this time he was going to be more adventurous and try out backpacking on his own in New Zealand, without friends or family as contacts as he had in Scotland.

Backpacking in New Zealand
He started his trip in Christchurch, and explored the South Island which he thought was beautiful.

He even tried out for the casting of the 'Lord of the Rings', being filmed then in New Zealand, with some friends he'd met up with, but none of them were successful. He did some short bus tours and at Queenstown tried sky-diving and bungee jumping. He even tried the sky swing at Queenstown which blew him away and left him speechless.

'In New Zealand, I felt comfortable. I could just be myself. I didn't have to explain myself all the time.'

Then, in Dunedin, his passport was stolen. That was stressful but the British embassy was very helpful and he had a replacement passport within a few hours. Being able to manage this situation himself made him feel confident.

He continued to call home most days, wanting to know what was happening there.

Knowing my limitations
Managing his epilepsy was a little more challenging and led to some situations.

'I found myself in a pub in Palmerston North (on the North Island of New Zealand) on the night of the FA Cup Final (English Football). I was talking to a mate I'd met called Andy Skinner.

Kim and Pim, two travelling friends, with Steven at Kitty O'Shea's pub in Wellington.

He thought I was vulnerable travelling around by myself, which offended me a little bit. After the game finished, he and his mates wanted to escort me back to the Youth Hostel where I was staying so I let them. It made them feel good and I didn't want to make an issue of it.

At the Immigrant Hotel in Auckland

'A week or so later I was in Auckland, at a pub called "The Immigrant". I met a young Maori girl and we were just dancing together. Her father was there, too, and he was a bit cautious about me. In the end, he dragged her off. As she was going, she handed me her drink. I asked what it was but she just said it would make me feel good, so I drank it, even though I was thinking that I should not have.

'I should have had better judgment. I was walking along Queen Street the next day when I felt a seizure coming on. It's different for everyone who has epilepsy. For me, it's usually coloured lights and light flashes in my eyes. I knew I was going to need help very soon so I turned into the next pub I came to which happened to be the "Playhouse Pub".

'I couldn't see anything when I walked in but I heard someone shout saying, "Hey, Stevie!". It was Andy from Palmerston North and I felt a rush of gratitude that there was someone who could help me.

'"Look mate, sorry to put this on you, but I'm going to have a seizure. Can you help me out?" I said to him and explained that he just needed to get furniture out of the way so I wouldn't hurt myself. In the end, we had enough time to make it back to my room at the Youth Hostel, which was a shared room with bunk beds. I lay down on my bed and they called an ambulance.

'There was an Asian guy asleep in one of the beds and he woke up to see paramedics in the room attending to me.
He looked really confused.

'I went to the hospital and stayed there a few hours under observation. They said I couldn't go home unless I had someone come to pick me up. I said I would have to fly someone over from Australia and that wasn't going to happen. Finally, I asked to see a doctor. When the doctor came, I said to her, "Listen to what I am saying. Don't judge me for what you think I am, what you want me to be or what you think I am capable of." I spoke to her for five or ten minutes and convinced her that I was fully aware of my responsibilities, capabilities and knew what was going on. Finally, I said, "Can I leave?"

'"On one condition", she said. "You don't go back to the pub."

'"Are you joking?" I said. "That's the first place I am going!" She was shocked.

"What do you mean?"

"I'm going back there to buy those people that helped me a drink!" I replied.

When I got to the pub, Andy and his mates were shocked to see me. They weren't used to this. They wouldn't let me buy them a drink and the guy behind the bar said he wasn't serving me any alcohol. That was fine. I was happy drinking lemonade. I knew my limitations in the circumstances.'

Andy Skinner and friends at the Playhouse Hotel, two hours after Steven's release from hospital.

Steven and Jarrod at Nelson

Steven also had an opportunity to help someone with a disability who was being bullied.

'I was in a pub in Nelson and there was a bloke there who looked seriously intellectually disabled. He was pulling faces and making gestures and everyone was just trying to get him out of there. They were saying, "Why don't you go home?" or "Why don't you get a taxi?" He came up to me and said, 'Steven, I'm just like you. Help me out please." So, in a very loud voice, I called out, "Right you lot, f--- off and leave him alone." No-one went near him again. Later, he just walked off and I never saw him again but I felt like I'd proved his point.'

Returning to Australia with photos of the sights of New Zealand (not many) and photos of new friends he had made (lots), Steven believed he was ready to tackle back-packing in Europe.

Europe – I was very responsible
Six months after his New Zealand trip, he flew to Scotland again to catch up with friends and family before he tackled Europe.

His former primary school in Rosyth had burnt down a few years earlier with a brand new one built to replace it. He decided to visit it to see if any of his former teachers were there. When he got there, he found security was pretty tight. Since the Dunblane massacre in 1996, when a man had walked into a Scottish primary school-shooting sixteen students, no-one could just walk into a school anymore. Steven spoke to the secretary in the office through an intercom and asked if his Grade Six teacher was still there. The secretary said she was but Steven wasn't allowed to come in and see her. Steven, full of cheek, said, "Then please ask her to come down to the gate to see me." Steven must have made quite an impression on his teacher because she did just that, bringing her class with her to speak to Steven and catch up with him.

L to R – Uncle Bill, Steven, Aunt Edna, Jane (Steven's mum), Claire and David in front.

On this trip, Steven was able to finally meet up with his mother again, whom he hadn't seen since he was three years old, and meet his step-brother and sisters.

As well as his schoolmates and family in Scotland, Steven had new contacts in the United Kingdom and Europe to catch up with from his backpacking days in New Zealand. He wasn't fazed about travelling in non-English speaking countries and organized his European trips himself.

'I was very responsible and sensible about my own safety. I wasn't going to take foolish risks.' As on his other trips, he rang home to Australia almost every day. His family always had an approximate idea of where he was.

He went to France on one trip, travelling by train. At Flandres Station in Lille, he was having a communication difficulty buying a ticket to Amsterdam to visit some friends he had met in New Zealand. A girl further back in the queue asked in English if she could help him. The ticket sorted, he started chatting and found out she was from Geelong.

'Get away! Go right over there and don't talk to me ever again!' he said.

'Why?' she asked. He slapped his identification card on the counter and she realized he was from Geelong, too. They had a hug and went back to her flat for coffee and chocolate. They started sharing connections. She had relatives who had worked at the Happy Hens egg farm whom Steven remembered. When he came home from Europe, they stayed in touch. These coincidences happened to Steven constantly in his travels.

I could hear music blaring
He was also careful with his money and this 'carefulness' led to one of his biggest adventures.

'I was travelling by train from Krakow in Poland to Graz in Austria to visit a friend I had met in Wellington, New Zealand. I needed to change trains at Bruck in Austria, so when we pulled into the station I was looking for signs or some sort of direction but I took too long and the train pulled out of the station with me still aboard. Next thing I knew, the conductor was coming down the aisle, screaming at me in German. He said Bruck was the last station on my ticket and I would have to pay 200 Euros extra and travel on to Venice. I didn't want to do that so I got off at the next stop, which was Leoben.

'Leoben is a university city. When the train stopped there, it was 2:30 in the morning. The platforms were deserted and no-one was in the station area. So, I picked up my back pack, bought a Coke at a vending machine and sat down to wonder what I could do. Where could I find accommodation at that time of the morning?

'Outside the station, I could hear music blaring. That was strange for a Monday night, I thought. I followed the sound to what looked like a town hall where there seemed to be a sort of party going on. I could see people dancing inside. I asked the bouncer on the door, "Is this a private party?"

'He said, "Yes, it is a University party." I found out later it was run every last Monday night of the month with council approval. He let me in and inside there was a guy head-banging to Australian rock group AC/DC's "Highway to Hell". I took his photo and we started talking. He said he had back-packed from South Africa. I said I was Scottish but living in Australia now. I told him my story about missing my train stop.

'"Come and stay at my place. I like helping people out." When I asked him why he would do that, he said I should pass it on to someone else in the future.

'"Okay", I said, "I can go with that." A Metallica song came on, "Enter Sandman". "Wicked! Metallica!" I said. He said there was going to be a concert in two days time at the Aerodrome in Vienna as part of a two day rock festival and he said he might be able to get me a ticket. I'd have to find somewhere to sleep but I told him I'd find somewhere – I had tonight.

'My friend's name was Harold Schmidt. It turned out that some of the people in the group didn't think much of him but he was good to me. For example, my bank card was cracked and wouldn't work so he helped me fix it with tape.

'In the end, the ticket fell through but I really wanted to go to the festival so I caught a bus from Leoben Station to where the festival was being held. I bought my ticket, leaving my back-pack in a huge shipping container near the gate and went in to enjoy the music. I came back at midnight, collected my back-pack and headed off to the camping ground, looking for somewhere to stay. I'd bought a bed sheet at a stall during the day. I thought that, at worst, I could sleep on the grass.

'I came across a tent with a sunshade awning and a table in it, so I lay down under the table with the sheet pulled over me and my backpack. A girl came out of a tent and asked me what I was doing so I explained I had nowhere to stay and would it be okay if I slept there for the night? She said she would check with her friends who owned the tent and came back to say it would be okay. I was very glad about that because there was torrential rain for the next two days. I actually overheard them talking about me, that I snored the first night but then someone else said I had nowhere else to stay so they kindly let me stay there.

*At the Aerodrome Festival in Vienna.
These people let Steven sleep in their area.*

'Several years later, on another trip, I visited Leoben again and decided to look up Harold Schmidt. It turned out he wasn't living in Leoben anymore. A lady in the administration office at the University called and left a message for me at his new number and I was chuffed when one of the ladies at the University café remembered me.'

Don't go to Bulgaria
On this trip, Steven decided to extend his travels to Eastern Europe.

'Various backpackers I met said not to go to Bulgaria because it's too scary and people get into trouble there. I like doing what people say I can't do, so I went there anyway.' He went alone by train and got off at the main station in Sofia. He caught a taxi to the backpacker's hostel but when the taxi charged too much he thought it might be better not to argue this time.

'Once I'd booked in, I went for a walk around the streets nearby and came across an Irish pub, called "O'Neil's", I think. I drank there for the next three or four evenings after touring during the day, even though a lot of the clientele seemed very strange. The Bulgarian bouncer spoke English and one evening he said to me, "Do you feel safe in this pub?"

'"Why wouldn't I?" I said. "I'm just having a pint."

'"This is a Mafia pub", he said. I kept going there, though, because there was a very pretty barmaid there. I was flirting with her a bit, even though I knew she was out of my league.

'One night, I took some friends from the hostel where I was staying. One of them started demanding his drink be free because they couldn't change the note he was offering them. Knowing the clientele, I said, "I'll pay for the beer. Don't worry." It wasn't worth it to cause trouble there.'

Steven enjoyed meeting new people, travelling and seeing new places. When he had to, he would go to places alone, such as the time he went to the "Moulin Rouge" in Paris on his own. Increasingly, pubs were becoming the focal point when he came into a new town. It got to the stage where he was drinking six or seven hours a night with other backpackers. He remembers going to a night-club when he was "off his face" with alcohol. A bouncer pushed him over but he got straight back up, left and found a bus stop. He got back to the hostel at 7:30 am and slept all day. He wasn't taking in a lot of the sights living like this.

I always took my medication
At the same time, he refused all offers of drugs from other backpackers. He had his epilepsy medication with him and always took it to avoid seizures. On his European trip, he had taken a year's supply of medication with him. If he began

to feel tremors, then he would ease off the alcohol for a day or two. On the whole, his epilepsy wasn't a problem when he was travelling.

Having a disability had its advantages and disadvantages. There were times when Steven was quite capable of using the sympathy people felt because of what they perceived as his disability to get himself out of trouble. On the other hand, there were a few occasions when he was targeted because people thought he might be an easy touch. For example, he was drinking in a pub in Ilford, Essex, with his uncle. After his uncle left, Steven stayed on a while longer and was quite inebriated when he left. He went to a taxi office where the driver demanded £15 up front. When Steven opened his wallet, the man snatched all his money and gestured to Steven to follow him but Steven walked off. Eventually he found another taxi rank and gained the sympathy of a passenger waiting there, who dropped him off where he was staying, refusing to accept any payment.

On another occasion, he had to find his way home in a strange city. This happened in Nottingham, England.

'I went to a pub with some guys I had met (just random guys) to watch soccer. It got boring once the game had finished so I left. There was a taxi outside with two girls in the back (they turned out to be Irish). I opened the front door and asked if they were going to the city and asked if I could share the taxi. They said okay, but once I was sitting in the front seat, they started carrying on from the back seat, saying, 'Who are you? What are your motives? How can we trust you?' I wasn't going to put up with that so when the taxi stopped at the traffic lights, I got out. I had no idea where I was.

Next thing I know, the taxi has gone around the square and pulled up beside me. They opened the door and said they were just joking so I ended up getting in again and going to a night-club with them.

When I was ready to leave the night-club, I went outside. It was the early hours of the morning and I had no idea where I was. I spent about twenty minutes asking people if they knew the way to the youth hostel I was staying at, but no-one could help. Finally, I was able to get a taxi back there. He never had any physical attacks in his travels. He believes his street-smarts helped protect him.

"You just have to keep your wits about you," he says.

Steven with the two girls he met in Nottingham.

Travelling Australia
After Steven returned again to Australia, he decided it was time to see more of the country where he lived. In 2006, he took a trip to Adelaide and once there booked a 'Groovy Grape Tour' which was a bus trip to Alice Springs. He didn't

Above, Adelaide to Alice Springs on the 'Groovy Grape' bus tour.

think much of Alice Springs. 'It was pretty desolate'.

He struck up a friendship of sorts with a Japanese girl, Yuko, who was travelling by herself around Australia. It took about a week to get to Alice Springs and they slept in backpacker hostels in the small towns along the way.

Back in Geelong for a while, he stayed in touch with Yuko. They met up again in Adelaide and travelled to Perth on the Overland train, a trip of three days and two nights. There was a three hour stopover at Kalgoorlie and Steven went on a three hour pub crawl. He was so drunk they almost didn't let him back on the train but he threw his arms around a guy he recognized from his carriage and pretended this guy was Steven's carer, so they let him on.

Yuko didn't like his drinking, so Steven didn't drink when he was just with her. They travelled to Broome together from Perth, at times hitch-hiking for part of the way. By the time they got to Broome, Steven was ready to go his own way. He had met up with some other travelling friends along the way and didn't want to spend all his time with Yuko.

Steven and Yuko in Alice Springs

He told Yuko he was going to travel on by himself and she was quite upset, which upset Steven, but it was what he needed to do.

Clare
Steven took a bus ride to Darwin, staying at a backpacker's hostel. He bumped into two backpackers he had met previously, Clare from England and Denis from Ireland. Steven got on well with Clare especially, a friendship that continues to this day. He moved to their hostel and spent time exploring Darwin with them.

Steven was still phoning home most days and knew his younger brother was about to play in a soccer final. He decided to surprise him and flew back for the game, which his brother's team won.

On the move again, he flew to Cairns where he met up with Clare and Denis again. They ended up staying in Port Douglas for a few weeks. Back in Cairns, Steven developed an ear infection and had to go to hospital in Cairns by ambulance, a trip that cost $800. He had thought it must be another seizure. Just after his hospital treatment, while he was drinking in a bar with Denis, he collapsed. The medication he had in his system was still affecting him. The police came but Steven talked his way out of it.

'We had good times, good fun.' Steven found that Claire was a very good friend and he felt a strong attachment to her. He spent time in Sydney with her, but then she had to return to England because she was homesick and Steven returned to Geelong.

Two years later, Clare returned to Australia, working in Melbourne for a time so she and Steven were able to spend time together again. In the end, she needed to return to her family in England and

Steven needed to stay living independently in Geelong. They continue to stay in touch by telephone every few days so the friendship continues. Maybe one of them will visit the other one day, but that is how things stand for now.

Travelling was empowering for Steven. He managed well what others said he couldn't do. He got to know his mother's family, revived his childhood friendships and met many new people that he still counts as friends. He travelled all through Europe, New Zealand and Australia, coping with the minor crises that came his way and not letting his disabilities stop him from doing what he wanted to do.

It also helped him realise that, while he was Scottish, Australia was now home for him and likely to be in the future.

10. MAKING CHANGES

Good coffee
Back home in Australia, Steven's life was based around watching his local soccer team and spending time at local hotels where he had various friends he could meet up with. This involved a fair amount of drinking, which was beginning to affect his health.

In 2008, he moved to Warrnambool for twelve months or so. In his travels around Australia, he had met a particular young lady who worked as a barmaid in Warrnambool and he decided it was time to try his chances with her. He rented a unit and arranged for his support services to continue there. After a while, he realised he was a lot keener than the young lady was.

Meanwhile, he had developed a friendship with the lady who cleaned his home in Warrnambool and they had a brief relationship. She preferred coffee shops to pubs, so Steven began to develop an appreciation for good coffee. Then she moved interstate, so that ended the friendship, although they parted on good terms.

In a bad place
Unexpectedly, Steven had an unusual seizure that placed him in hospital in Warrnambool for a couple of days. As a result of the seizure, Steven's impairment on his left side was accentuated and he lost some peripheral vision. He decided it was time to return to Geelong again so he moved back and rented a unit in the centre of town.

He continued drinking at his local pubs but he was developing some mental health issues. Around this time, he remembers being offered some work by a concreter he had met at a local hotel called 'Irish Murphy's'. He stuck with this job for three weeks but he felt very uncomfortable with the comments made by some of his co-workers. He decided to leave because he realised that he was in a bad place. He was depressed, his health was deteriorating and it was time to do something about it.

After a severe bout of the flu, and with constant warnings from his doctor, Steven decided it was time to give up alcohol. This was a big decision because it meant not going to hotels which cut off many of his social contacts during the week. This was a huge change in his life. It meant being home alone most nights with the television for company instead of being with other people in a bar.

There wasn't a lot to do during the day and at night he had nothing to do. Very little of what was on television interested him. He could see that his depression was becoming worse and he was increasingly paranoid. Things were looking very dark. He decided the only thing to do was to voluntarily admit himself to the Geelong Clinic.

New strategies
The Geelong Clinic is a mental health hospital that provides high quality psychiatric care. Steven stayed just for a week, but made changes as a result of that stay that have made big improvements to his life.

Firstly, he got Foxtel connected to his television. This gave him a wider variety of programs to watch, such as the heavy rock music he enjoyed and more sport, especially soccer. There were also other series that appealed to him not shown on the free to air channels. It gave him something to do in the evenings.

'One of the strategies for coping with my mental health issues that I learnt at Geelong Clinic was to use music. If I was alone in the house, I could use music to create a presence. Foxtel gave me music channels to choose from. I also enjoyed watching sport.'

Secondly, he was put in touch with St Laurence Services. He began attending some of their day programs, such as the ABI Social Group, which goes on outings once a week, and men's group lunches. This gave him new social contacts and he felt that he was able to give advice and support to some of his fellow ABI sufferers. He also developed friendly relationships with some of the staff working for St Laurence, exercising his wit on them, and debating whatever the topic of the day was. Some of these discussions led to him helping initiate a Tuesday night bowling group run by St Laurence that is now very popular.

Becoming a regular at some of the coffee shops, he also developed contacts there and had places to go where he felt he was personally welcomed. His week began to have a structure. On weekdays he went to St Laurence programs. He had a meal with family members most Monday nights. He went bowling Tuesday nights. At the weekend, he went to the movies and out for meals with groups of friends. He also watched his brother play soccer with his family. It took time, but he now had a new network of people where he felt valued and where he could make a contribution.

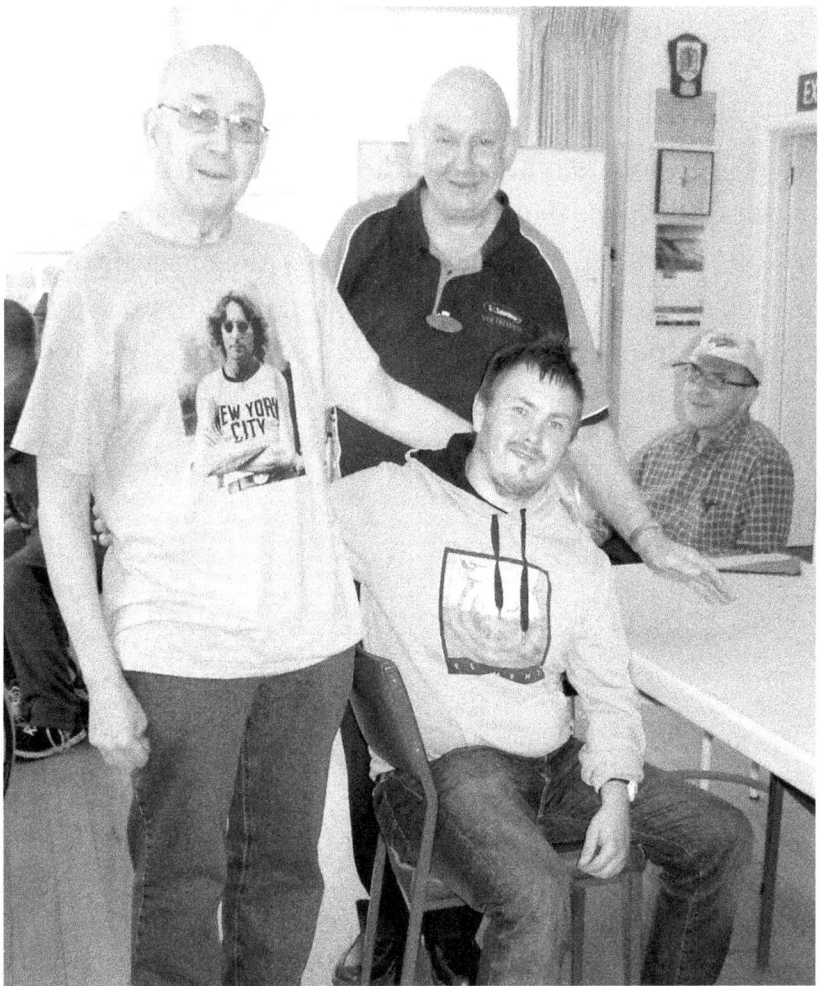

Lunch at St Laurence's Men's group. L to R- Robin, Andy standing behind Steven and Digger seated.

He continues to have a strong relationship with his father. As well, he speaks regularly to his mother in England and stays in touch with other friends in England and Scotland.

Steven was thinking about his future in a new way. He often says, 'Loneliness is the price of independence'. He can cope with the periods of loneliness now, but he doesn't want living alone to be permanent. He feels ready to settle down with the right person.

I'll take some water next time
Meanwhile, he does his best to enjoy life, even if he has to do some things alone. Recently, Steven returned from a brief holiday in Canberra by himself. He organised his hotel and flight bookings through a travel agency.

After visiting the War Memorial and the Questacon Science Centre, there wasn't a lot else for him to do. Canberra didn't seem to have the same coffee shop culture as they have in Melbourne or Geelong, so he settled for watching some soccer in the bar of the hotel, drinking coke. He heard some people talking about walking to the top of Mt Ainslie. Located near the War Memorial, Mt Ainslie is part of a nature park in Canberra and is just over 800 metres high. You can drive to the lookout at the top and get panoramic views of the city but there are also walking tracks, two to three kilometers long, which are quite steep and challenging. Although it was steeper than Steven expected, he made it to the top and joined others enjoying the view. Somehow, he missed the path on the way back and ended up 'bush-bashing', hanging on to trees in steep descents and getting totally lost. After two hours of this, he ended up in a ravine where going up or down seemed equally bad options. His legs and arms were scratched and his clothes were torn. He was also badly dehydrated because he hadn't brought any water with him. He decided it was time to call for help.

He hadn't told anyone at the hotel where he was going or that he had epilepsy. Thankfully, he had his phone with him, Googled the hotel's number and told the receptionist what had happened. The manager and another staff member came to find him, calling out for him in the bush. They needed to support him as he they walked him back down to their car.

Steven likes to manage his situations himself if he can but getting lost in the bush was definitely outside his limits and more than he could cope with on his own. Should he have taken the walk to the top of Mount Ainslie? Yes, he thinks he should have, but he should have taken water and he should have asked other people walking the track to check he took the right path down.

Doing things alone means taking risks and Steven says he has no intention of slowing down. Next time, though, he'll take better precautions.

11. LIFE CHANGES

There is much more to me than people realise
The accident Steven had when he was sixteen years old changed his life forever, but some of the changes have been good ones. His courage and tenacity have helped him to make a good life for himself in spite of his injuries. The accident stopped him heading into a life of petty crime: several of his teenage friends ended up spending life in jail. Instead, he is able to make a contribution to the people in his life and the groups he is involved in.

Two years ago, Steven agreed to be a participant in the 'Living Book Project'. This is a project where volunteers with a disability can be 'borrowed' for fifteen minutes or so in order that people can talk to them and better understand what their lives are like. Steven worked with Anna Loughry, a social worker at St Laurence, to develop his 'Book notes'.

I visited the 'Living Book Project' and saw for myself how well he handled speaking to various people about his life.

He prepared with Anna an introductory brochure about him as a Living Book. Here are some quotes:

"I am a proud fellow who tries to treat everyone with respect and believe that people have the same rights to respect regardless of their abilities / disabilities."

"I have lived independently since I was 20. There is much more to me than people realise."

"What part does humour play in my life? It makes me happy. I can make jokes to deflect attention when it's something I don't want to talk about. It's just how I cope."

"Do people treat me differently because I have a disability? I find that difficult to answer because I don't have the experience of being treated as a 'non-disabled' adult. What it comes down to for me is being treated with a negative or a positive attitude."

"People tend to put me in the "disabled" box until they take the time to know me. Once they get to know me then I am willing to share my true feelings with them."

"I feel like I have no other option now than to be positive, even though it's hard sometimes to find positives. I need to accept things don't always go my way. I need to try and rise above prejudices so that life does not get on top of me."

His confidence in advocating for people with a disability, not just on his own behalf, has grown considerably. He has participated in the Living Book Project several times now.

He has also successfully followed through with an Equal Opportunity claim with a restaurant that refused him service in the middle of the day because they thought he was drunk. He wasn't. They just jumped to conclusions.

Steven's journey is far from over. His health will continue to present challenges. I am confident, though, that he will cope with whatever these challenges are because, as Steven's uncle said, 'Steven is Steven.'

NOTES

CHAPTER ONE
1.1 The accounts in this chapter are based on testimony given on 8/5/1992 <u>Inquest into the Death of Steven Michael Kelly</u> 6/92 (84) Geelong Coroner's Court.

CHAPTER THREE
3.1 Exhibit G, 8/5/1992 <u>Inquest into the Death of Steven Michael Kelly</u> 6/92 (84) Geelong Coroner's Court.
3.2 Deposition given by Senior Constable Trevor Purcell, ibid.
3.3 Coroner's findings, ibid.

CHAPTER FOUR
4.1 *Geelong Advertiser*, Friday, January 10, 1992.
4.2 *Geelong Advertiser,* Friday, Monday, January 13, 1992

CHAPTER SIX
6.1 Website of Brain Injury Australia, <u>http://www.braininjuryaustralia.org.au/</u>, accessed 17 May 2014.
6.2 'About Acquired Brain Injury', <u>http://www.braininjuryaustralia.org.au/index.php</u>

?option=com_content&view=article&id=2&Itemid=3 , accessed 17 May 2014.
6.3 ibid.

CHAPTER SEVEN
7.1 The History of St Laurence Services, http://www.stlaurence.org.au/about/history.aspx accessed 23 May 2013.

USEFUL LINKS

1. BRAIN INJURY AUSTRALIA
Brain Injury Australia is the peak acquired brain injury (ABI) advocacy body representing, through its State and Territory Member Organisations, the needs of people with an acquired brain injury, their families and carers. Its website has a web links page to organisations throughout Australia. It also has a list of useful fact sheets to download.
Website: http://www.braininjuryaustralia.org.au/
Telephone: 9808 9390   Freecall: 1800 272 461

 Address: Suite 5, Hodson Building

     Royal Rehabilitation Centre Sydney

     241 Morrison Rd, Putney NSW 2112

2. BRAINLINK SERVICES

BrainLink Services is a Victorian based service that is dedicated to improving the quality of life of people affected by acquired disorders of the brain. The services BrainLink offer include a first point of call for families at onset of diagnosis and a range of support programs, including help with navigating the service sector.

Website: http://www.brainlink.org.au/

Telephone: 1800 677 579 (toll free)

Address: BrainLink Services Limited

54 Railway Road

Blackburn Victoria 3130

Australia

3. ST LAURENCE SERVICES

St Laurence Services offers a range of community services in south-western Victoria, including programs for people with brain injuries.

Website: www.stlaurence.org.au/

Telephone: 03 5282 1405

Address: St Laurence services have several locations, including in Geelong, Ballarat and Colac. The head office address is located at

90 Station Lake Road,

Lara. Victoria 3212

www.ingramcontent.com/pod-product-compliance
Lightning Source LLC
Chambersburg PA
CBHW071306040426
42444CB00009B/1892